#45
Mark Twain Branch Library
9621 S. Figueroa Street
Los Angeles, CA 90003

READY FOR MILITARY ACTION

FORTY-FIVE

AWESOME
MILITARY ROBOTS

by Carla Mooney

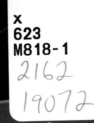

Content Consultant
George A. Bekey
Professor of Computer Science Emeritus
University of Southern California

Core Library

An Imprint of Abdo Publishing
www.abdopublishing.com

www.abdopublishing.com

Published by Abdo Publishing, a division of ABDO, PO Box 398166, Minneapolis, Minnesota 55439. Copyright © 2015 by Abdo Consulting Group, Inc. International copyrights reserved in all countries. No part of this book may be reproduced in any form without written permission from the publisher. Core Library™ is a trademark and logo of Abdo Publishing.

Printed in the United States of America, North Mankato, Minnesota
092014
012015

Cover Photo: Andrea Sutherland (Fort Carson)/US Department of Defense
Interior Photos: Andrea Sutherland (Fort Carson)/US Department of Defense, 1; Sgt. Kimberly Hackbarth/US Army, 4; US Navy, 7; US Marine Corps/Department of Defense, 8; US Army, 9, 20, 25; Sgt. Sarah Dietz/DVIDS, 11; AP Images, 12, 15; Stefan Rousseau/AP Images, 17; Ed Bailey/Corbis Images, 18, 45; Rebecca Craig/AP Images, 23; Larry Downing/Corbis Images, 28; Department of Defense, 32; David Howells/Corbis Images, 34; Erik Hildebrandt/US Navy, 36; Master Sgt. Shane A. Cuomo/US Air Force, 40; Lee Jin-man/AP Images, 38 (left); Northrop Grumman/UPI/Newscom, 38 (right); Photographer's Mate 1st Class Robert R. McRill, 42; Yoichi Hayashi/AP Images, 43

Editor: Patrick Donnelly
Series Designer: Becky Daum

Library of Congress Control Number: 2014944239

Cataloging-in-Publication Data
Mooney, Carla.
 Awesome military robots / Carla Mooney.
   p. cm. -- (Ready for military action)
ISBN 978-1-62403-649-1 (lib. bdg.)
Includes bibliographical references and index.
1. Military robots--United States--Juvenile literature. 2. United States--Armed Forces--Robots--Juvenile literature.   I. Title.
623--dc23
                                              2014944239

CONTENTS

CHAPTER ONE

SAVING LIVES

During the wars in Iraq and Afghanistan in the early 2000s, a machine called Scooby Doo showed the value of military robots. Scooby Doo worked with US troops in an explosive ordnance disposal (EOD) team. EOD teams work to disable roadside bombs called improvised explosive devices (IEDs). Those bombs have been a dangerous threat for soldiers in Iraq and Afghanistan.

Troops practice climbing rubble with an iRobot Packbot 510 during a robotics class at Fort Irwin, California.

Hull BUG

The US Navy is developing an underwater robot to clean its ships. Small marine animals called barnacles grow on ship hulls. Too many barnacles cause the ship to move slower in the water and use more fuel. The new robot, called a Hull BUG, is less than three feet (1 m) long and weighs only 50 pounds (23 kg). It uses an attachment that scrapes a ship's hull clean. On the Hull BUG's underside, a spinning propeller creates suction against the ship's hull. This allows the BUG to stay firmly attached to the ship. The navy plans to use the BUG robot to make its ships more efficient as they sail the world's oceans.

Robots such as Scooby Doo are some of an EOD unit's most valuable tools. Scooby Doo was a type of Packbot. This robot weighs 60 pounds (27 kg). It has four cameras and an articulated arm with a gripper. It also has flippers that allow it to travel over stairs and other obstacles. It can even use its flippers to turn itself over. Soldiers use Packbots for spy missions and surveillance. They also send the robots to find and dispose of bombs.

The Hull BUG uses a biofilm detector to differentiate between clean and unclean surfaces on the hull of a ship.

Other Packbot robots are even smaller than Scooby. They can weigh as little as 40 pounds (18 kg) and fit into a soldier's backpack. Packbots have a built-in satellite tracking system. They also have a compass and temperature sensors. They move on small treads at speeds of more than eight miles per hour (13 km/h).

A Packbot usually goes into a dangerous area before the troops. Soldiers operate the robot with a radio control unit. The control unit is like a laptop

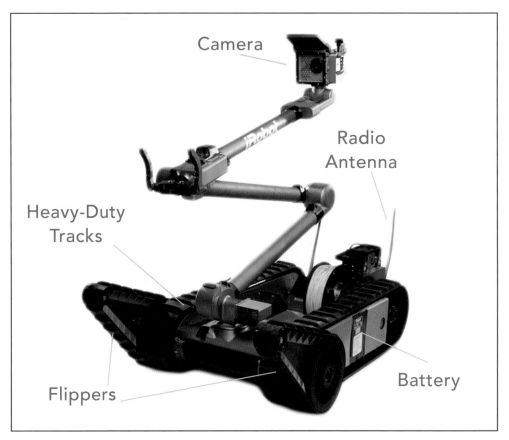

Packbot Explorer

Packbot robots are used for many military missions. How does each part of the Packbot assist during a mission?

computer with a gaming controller. Soldiers use the controller to move the robot from a distance.

Mechanical Eyes, Ears, and Nose

The robot carries a camera and several sensors. The camera sends back pictures to the EOD team. It works

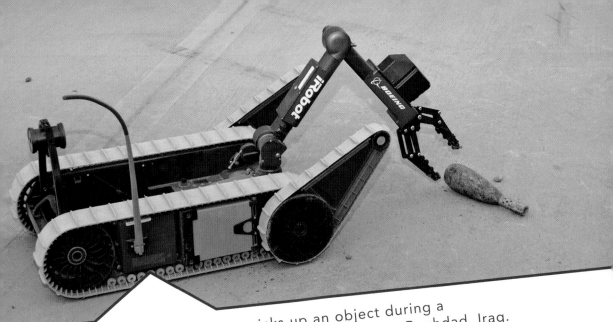

An iRobot Packbot picks up an object during a demonstration at Victory Base Complex, Baghdad, Iraq.

in all types of lighting, from bright sun to dark night. Some Packbot robots have sensors that can pick up different scents and sounds. These sensors can alert soldiers to dangerous gases, hazardous materials, and IEDs. The Packbot's arm can lift 30-pound (14-kg) loads. It can also place bomb disrupters on IEDs that fire jets of water to detach their triggers.

Scooby on the Job

In Iraq soldiers used Scooby Doo to dispose of 17 IEDs and one car bomb. Every time the robot completed a successful mission, the soldiers drew a line on its head unit to keep track. On Scooby's last mission, the EOD team attempted to defuse an IED. It exploded and destroyed the robot. A soldier took Scooby to the repair unit at Camp Victory, near Baghdad, Iraq. He asked the repair technicians to fix Scooby. But too much damage had been done. The little robot that had saved many lives could not be repaired. Scooby was retired from duty.

Scooby Doo is now on display at iRobot headquarters in Bedford, Massachusetts. iRobot is the company that makes Packbot robots like

Donkey Robots

The US Marines may soon use a robotic donkey to carry supplies. Scientists from Boston Dynamics, an engineering company, are working to develop the robot. The LS3, or Legged Squad Support System, is built to be a pack mule for soldiers on a march. The large robot donkey has four legs. It can carry as much as 400 pounds (180 kg) through rough terrain. The LS3 can also charge radios and handheld devices.

The LS3 is a robot with legs that can haul equipment for US troops.

Scooby. A plaque dedicated to Scooby is next to the display.

Today, thousands of unmanned robots work in the air and on the ground for the US military. These robots are perfect for jobs that are dull, dirty, and dangerous. Soldiers use robots to explore hazardous areas and investigate threats. They operate robots to find and disarm IEDs. Using robots keeps soldiers safe from harm.

CHAPTER TWO

ROBOTS IN THE MILITARY

obots seem like a very modern type of technology. But they actually have a long history in the military. The first robots used in combat appeared in World War I (1914–1918). That war pitted a group of countries led by Germany against the United States, the United Kingdom, and other allied nations. In 1916 the Germans put a wireless radio control system into a motorboat.

The German robot Goliath was a feared weapon during World War II.

Dragon Runner

The Dragon Runner robot was developed for the US Marine Corps in 2004. It moves on four wheels and weighs approximately 14 pounds (6 kg). It fits into a soldier's backpack. The Dragon Runner helps marine units see around corners and obstacles. It has cameras, sensors, motion detectors, and listening devices. The Dragon Runner sends the marines a picture of the hostile area before human troops enter. The robot's operator can move its arm to lift any small objects it finds.

Lightning Bug

In the 1960s the US military developed an unmanned reconnaissance aircraft called the Model 147 Lightning Bug. It flew over Southeast Asia during US involvement in the Vietnam War from 1962 to 1975. During that time the aircraft flew more than 3,000 missions. On some missions the Lightning Bug took photos of enemy camps. Other times the aircraft acted as a decoy or jammed enemy radar.

Pioneer Drones

In the Persian Gulf War (1990–1991) the US military flew an unmanned aerial vehicle (UAV) called the

The Dragon Runner is a versatile robot that can be carried in a soldier's backpack.

Pioneer. The navy flew the Pioneer over enemy territory to find targets. Then battleship guns fired at the targets. On one mission, a group of Iraqi soldiers waved white sheets of surrender when a Pioneer drone flew overhead. It was the first time that soldiers surrendered to an unmanned robot.

Precision Systems

In 1995 the introduction of GPS allowed the military to use unmanned drones more precisely. Soldiers could send a UAV with GPS anywhere in the world.

Crew members aboard the battleship USS Wisconsin prepare a Pioneer UAV for launch.

The US military used two new UAVs during the 1999 Kosovo conflict. They were the RQ-1 Predator and the RQ-4 Global Hawk. These drones carried cameras and sensors that gathered real-time, detailed information for military units.

Military engineers built on the knowledge they gained from these robots. They continued improving the technology and found new uses for them. Today the US military has some of the most powerful and innovative robots in the world.

In this 2012 interview, Jorgen David Pedersen, founder of robotics engineering firm RE2 Inc., talked about the future of military robots:

> Q: Do you envision a day where man and robot fight side by side on our frontlines?
>
> A: In a way, man and robot are already fighting side by side today. However, the robot has the tougher end of the relationship! The robot is the one entering caves to gain reconnaissance information, for example, while the person remains at a known, safer location. How these robots fight side by side, however, will change and improve over time. . . . One of those scenarios [is] the "robotic wingman." In this scenario, the robot is like an intelligent robotic mule, carrying ammunition and supplies, mirroring the movements of dismounted troops, providing supplies to those who need it, etc.

Source: "Robotics in the Military: Jorgen David Pedersen of RE2, Inc." Robotics Tomorrow. www.roboticstomorrow.com, January 31, 2012. Web. Accessed August 19, 2014.

What's the Big Idea?

Take a close look at this interview. What is Pedersen's main point about military robots now and in the future? Pick out two details he uses to make this point. What can you tell about military robots based on this interview?

CHAPTER THREE

SMALL ROBOTS

In dangerous areas, soldiers need to search for threats without risking harm. Small reconnaissance robots give soldiers a way to explore an unknown area from a safe distance. Soldiers can carry them into the field. They deploy the robots into an area to gather video and audio before human soldiers enter. Other small robots deliver weapons to soldiers in the field. Built-in sensors detect chemicals and other

The TALON robot's treads help it navigate all types of terrain.

Recon Scout

Sometimes the best way to get a robot into place is to throw it. The Recon Scout is a small robot. The entire system weighs approximately three pounds (1.4 kg) and is only eight inches (20 cm) long. It looks like a small barbell. It has wheels at each end of a titanium tube. The tube holds the robot's camera and sensors.

Soldiers can carry the robot in a vest or pouch. In seconds soldiers can throw the Scout over walls and through building windows. Then the robot sends video and sensor data from inside the building to soldiers outside. US troops have used the Recon Scout for surveillance missions in Iraq and Afghanistan.

dangers. And despite their small size, these robots are tough. They can travel over almost any terrain.

TALON

The TALON is a powerful yet lightweight robot. It weighs less than 100 pounds (45 kg). It can work day or night in all types of weather. The TALON moves on small treads that take it over stairs, through rubble, and even snow. It is also amphibious, which means it works on land and in the water. During one mission in Iraq, a TALON fell off a bridge and into a river.

Soldiers can throw the Recon Scout robot into potentially dangerous locations to provide vital surveillance.

The soldiers controlling the robot recovered it by simply driving it out of the water.

In the field, soldiers control the robot's movement with a joystick. The TALON has a mechanical arm and gripper to pick up objects. It is also equipped with sensors for nuclear, biological, and chemical weapons. The TALON's multiple cameras provide video surveillance. Soldiers use the cameras to search

Guardbot

The Guardbot is a robot, camera, and security system all in one sphere-shaped unit. The Guardbot's shape allows it to move easily across all types of terrain. It can be remotely controlled by an operator. It also can be programmed to follow GPS navigation. It carries two high-definition cameras that rotate 360 degrees and send back live images. The Guardbot also carries audio and radar sensors. The Guardbot's shell is sealed and waterproof so that it can be used in any weather. It even can float in water. In 2014 US Marines began testing the Guardbot for use in combat. It also has civilian uses. A Guardbot was used for surveillance during a soccer match in Mexico City, Mexico, in 2014.

for explosives and enemy troops.

The TALON was first used in 2000 in military operations in Bosnia. In Afghanistan and Iraq, these robots operated on thousands of missions to find IEDs. In the future the military may use the TALON to carry machine guns, rifles, and grenade launchers.

Packbot

The Packbot is a smaller robot that is often used in reconnaissance missions. It was first used in Iraq in 2003. Soldiers used its infrared and optical

The MARCbot IV can extend its camera to search for IEDs and examine suspicious items.

cameras to closely examine areas from a distance during the day or night. Packbots such as Scooby Doo protected human soldiers from unexpected booby traps or enemy soldiers.

MARCbot

At only 13.5 inches (34 cm) tall and weighing 35 pounds (16 kg), the MARCbot is one of the smallest and most commonly used military robots. US soldiers in Iraq regularly used the MARCbot to inspect suspicious objects. The robot helps troops identify IEDs from a safe distance. Soldiers can control the MARCbot from more than 300 feet (100 m) away. A low-light camera allows the robot to operate at night.

The MARCbot looks like a small toy truck on four wheels. It has a mechanical arm with a mounted camera. The camera sends back video images to remote soldiers. The camera can be raised and tilted. That allows soldiers to see over boxes and other obstacles. They can also look into trash cans or other receptacles.

Small robots perform many tasks on the battlefield. Sometimes, however, a job is too big for a small robot. That's when the US military's large robots are called to duty.

In this excerpt from a newspaper article, the author writes about research on soldiers' emotional attachment to robots:

> *When asked in the questionnaire and the interview, all participants unanimously defined a robot as a tool or a nonliving mechanical object. However, in their day-to-day interactions, [researcher Julie] Carpenter found that these personnel also socialized with the robot, with acts such as assigning gender pronouns, humorously naming them, and even having memorial services if the robot was destroyed. Another important finding was that the operators felt a sense of self-association with the robot, with it acting as "their hands" or a stand-in for them at a distance.*
>
> *"Some of the operators who specifically worked with robots operating on a daily basis suggested that they felt a sense of self in the robot, it almost acting like an avatar for themselves," she said.*

Source: Imana Gunawan. "UW Research Discovers Soldiers Can Develop Emotional Bonds to Robots." The Daily. University of Washington, October 9, 2013. Web. Accessed August 19, 2014.

Back It Up

The author of this passage is using evidence to support a point. Write a paragraph describing the point the author is making. Then write down two or three pieces of evidence the author uses to make the point.

CHAPTER FOUR

LARGE ROBOTS

Soldiers have to move many objects on the battlefield and in a military camp. They receive deliveries of weapons, ammunition, and supplies in remote locations. Injured soldiers are picked up and brought to base for medical attention. Traveling through dangerous areas puts human lives at risk. Using large robots to perform these tasks helps protect soldiers' lives.

The iRobot Warrior X700

Disaster Aid

In March 2011, a strong earthquake and tsunami hit Japan. The natural disasters damaged several nuclear reactors, creating a dangerous crisis. Inside one of the reactor's containment vessels, radiation levels were high enough to kill a person within minutes. During the disaster cleanup, two iRobot Warriors arrived to help. The high radiation levels did not affect the Warriors. The robots entered the dangerous area. They traveled across rubble and wreckage with industrial vacuums. The robots removed radioactive debris to reduce radiation levels. Using the Warriors instead of human relief workers saved lives.

ACER

For heavy-duty tasks, the Armored Combat Engineer Robot (ACER) is ready for the job. An ACER is the size of a small bulldozer. It weighs approximately 5,000 pounds (2,300 kg). The robotic vehicle is covered with steel armor to protect it from enemy fire.

A single soldier operates the ACER using a control unit and joysticks. The ACER has different attachments for different tasks. A plow blade or giant cutter allows the ACER to clear and cut down obstacles. With a minesweeper attachment, the ACER can clear a field of land mines. The ACER can tow disabled vehicles and carry cargo in a trailer.

M160

The M160 robot vehicle creates a safe path for soldiers. In Afghanistan, soldiers used the M160 to clear IEDs and unexploded weapons. It has a roller attached to its front with tools that churn the soil eight inches (20 cm) deep. The goal is to destroy or detonate mines. The M160 can withstand small explosions as it clears a minefield.

The M160 can also be used in other ways. On one mission in

ARTS

The All-Purpose Remote Transport System (ARTS) is built like a bulldozer. It can be used as a forklift, a backhoe, and a mine-clearing device. An operator remotely moves its mechanical arm to investigate suspicious packages. A water-jet tool can disarm explosives. Soldiers can operate an ARTS robot from up to three miles (4.8 km) away as long as it remains in sight.

Troops can customize the iRobot Warrior to perform a variety of tasks.

Afghanistan, an operator guided it approximately 30 yards (27 m) in front of a convoy's lead vehicle. On the route, a roadside bomb exploded and destroyed the M160. Although the robot was lost, the soldiers in vehicles behind it were safe.

iRobot Warrior 710

The iRobot Warrior is a powerful and rugged robot. It weighs approximately 500 pounds (230 kg). It can carry a load of up to 150 pounds (70 kg) for a variety of missions. The Warrior can transport hazardous materials and other heavy objects. Soldiers use it for search-and-rescue missions, surveillance, bomb disposal, and other tasks.

The Warrior can be customized for different missions. For some missions, soldiers fit a mechanical arm on the robot. The arm can lift more than 220 pounds (100 kg). It can open a car door or smash its way through a window. And it is strong enough to tow an entire car.

FURTHER EVIDENCE

Chapter Four contains a lot of information about large military robots. If you could pick out the main point of the chapter, what would it be? Find a few pieces of key evidence from the chapter that support the main point. Then explore the website below to learn even more about military robots. Find a quote from the website that supports the chapter's main point. Does the quote support an existing piece of evidence in the chapter? Or does it add a new piece of evidence? Why?

Driverless Convoy Demonstration
www.mycorelibrary.com/robots

FLYING ROBOTS

High in the sky, a Predator drone circles. The plane is too small and too far off the ground for anyone to hear or see it. The drone carries an infrared camera. It films everything it sees and sends video back to the pilot. The pilot sits in front of a computer screen and watches the video thousands of miles away. The plane is a UAV. The pilot uses a

The Predator drone is one of the US military's top UAVs.

The use of UAVs like this Global Hawk has sparked a debate about the role of drones in the US military.

satellite, computers, and a joystick to fly it by remote control.

The US military uses several UAVs, including the Predator. Some are small enough to be held by a soldier. Others are as big as a commercial airliner. Most UAVs are used for reconnaissance. Pilots fly them from a ground station that can be thousands of miles away. They use remote controls to steer the planes. UAVs can fly on the most dangerous missions. If the UAV is shot down, the pilot remains safe on the ground.

Some UAVs carry weapons. Operators use onboard cameras to find and identify a target. Then commanders can launch missiles or drop bombs from the UAV to attack the target.

Predator

First flown in 1994, the Predator is the most widely used UAV in combat.

Its engine is so quiet that it is almost impossible to hear it from the ground. It carries cameras, infrared sensors, and radar. The Predator takes pictures and video during the day or night. It can take pictures in any type of weather. The Predator's powerful cameras can

UAV Debate

Although many people in the military support the use of UAVs, others have concerns about the flying drones. Sometimes the military has the wrong information about a target's location. Other times innocent people are in the same area as a military target. When this occurs, civilians have been killed in UAV strikes. In addition, some people are concerned that operating a UAV is too much like a video game. UAV operators are far removed from the battlefield and the people being killed in UAV strikes. As a result critics of drone use wonder if the military is more likely to attack, even in times when a peaceful solution might be available.

	U-2 Spy Plane	Global Hawk
Wingspan	105 feet (32 m)	130.9 feet (40 m)
Length	63 feet (19 m)	47.6 feet (14.5 m)
Range*	8,000 miles (13,000 km)	14,000 miles (22,500 km)
Top Speed*	470 mph (760 km/h)	350 mph (560 km/h)
Highest Altitude*	70,000 feet (21,000 m)	60,000 feet (18,000 m)
Carrying Capacity*	5,000 pounds (2,300 kg)	3,200 pounds (1,500 kg)
Endurance*	10 hours	32 hours

*approximate values

Reconnaissance Then and Now

The US military has been using U-2 spy planes for reconnaissance missions since the 1950s. The Global Hawk UAV has taken over some of those jobs. How do the two aircraft compare to each other? What are the advantages and disadvantages of each?

zoom in a person's facial features from miles away. Back at their base, pilots can watch on a video screen and see what's happening on the ground.

Global Hawk

The Global Hawk is one of the largest UAVs used by the US military. It flies more than twice as high as the

Predator drone can fly. That makes it hard for the enemy to shoot it down. It also can watch a much wider area of the ground than smaller UAVs.

The Global Hawk is programmed to fly itself from takeoff to landing. Operators on the ground monitor the plane in the air. It can fly for more than a day without refueling. Because it can stay in the air for so long, the Global Hawk is a good fit for long surveillance missions.

The Global Hawk also has been used in peacetime missions. In 2011 the US Air Force flew it to Japan to assist in disaster relief and recovery after an earthquake and tsunami. The drone's sensors

Inspired by Nature

Engineers have developed a new drone inspired by a spinning maple seed. Like a maple seed, the Samarai flyer hovers with a single wing. A tiny jet engine provides thrust. A small flap on the edge of the wing controls its direction. The Samarai carries a camera that sends a 360-degree view to its operator. Weighing less than eight ounces (0.2 kg), the Samarai is perfect for secret missions in small, tight areas.

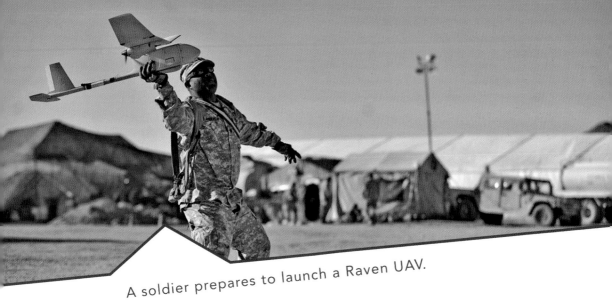

A soldier prepares to launch a Raven UAV.

were used to find passable roads and landing areas for relief operations. A Global Hawk also flew to help after the 2013 Philippines tsunami.

Raven

When soldiers on the ground need eyes in the sky, the Raven UAV is a useful tool. Small UAVs such as the Raven help soldiers on the ground see what waits over the next hill or around the corner. It helps them spot hidden enemies or explosive traps. Soldiers can launch a Raven by hand in minutes like a model airplane. It carries cameras and sensors that provide real-time video and data.

In many ways military robots help and protect soldiers every day. Whether big or small, on the ground or in the air, these robots are a valuable part of the US military.

EXPLORE ONLINE

Chapter Five discusses the use of UAVs in the US military. The website below further explores the use of UAVs. As you know, every source is different. What facts does the website give about UAVs? How is the information from the website the same as the information in Chapter Five? What new information did you learn from the website?

The Drones Come Home
www.mycorelibrary.com/robots

A TALON robot like this one helped the
search-and-rescue efforts at the WTC.

Searching the Rubble after 9/11

In the United States, TALON robots were also used to search for victims
in debris at the World Trade Center (WTC) after terrorists attacked
New York City on September 11, 2001. Emergency personnel used the
TALON robots extensively at Ground Zero, where the WTC towers fell.
The TALON robots proved to be extremely tough in difficult conditions.
They were the only robots at the WTC site to last through the entire
mission without needing a major repair.

Disaster Support

Some large military robots have helped during natural disasters. In 2011 a deadly earthquake and tsunami caused Japan's Fukushima nuclear power plant to melt down. The iRobot Warrior assisted in the massive cleanup. Warrior robots removed debris and measured radiation levels at the plant, protecting human lives.

Robots helped the recovery effort at the Fukushima nuclear plant.

Fighting Terrorists

In September 2011 armed drones operated by the US Central Intelligence Agency (CIA) took off from a secret US base in the Arabian Peninsula. They crossed into northern Yemen in the Middle East and fired missiles at a car. The targeted car carried several terrorist leaders, including Anwar al-Awlaki. He was accused of inspiring terrorists around the world and helping to plan several terrorist attacks. The car exploded, killing everyone inside.

Why Do I Care?

This book discusses how robots are used in the military. But robots are used in everyday life too. What types of robots have you seen in your community? How have engineers in the field of robotics improved our lives? Think about two or three ways the work of robots connects to your own life. Give examples of parts of your life that have been enhanced by robots.

Take a Stand

This book discusses robots and their contributions in the military. Critics have said that using robots instead of putting humans at risk makes the military more likely to attack its enemies rather than seek a peaceful resolution to a crisis. Take a position on the use of robots in the military and write a short essay detailing your opinion, reasons for your opinion, and facts and details that support those reasons.

Say What?

Find five words related to robots in this book that you have never seen or heard before. Find each word in a dictionary and read the definition. Rewrite the definition in your own words. Then use each word in a sentence.

Another View

Find another source about military robots. Write a short essay comparing and contrasting its point of view with that of this book's author. Be sure to answer these questions: What is the point of view of each author? How are they similar and why? How are they different and why?

GLOSSARY

articulated
having two or more sections connected by a flexible joint

defuse
to make a bomb safe so that it cannot explode

drone
a pilotless aircraft operated by remote control

infrared
light that cannot be seen by the human eye

mission
a special job or task for a military soldier or group

reconnaissance
a search for useful military information

satellite
a device that is launched into orbit around Earth

sensor
an instrument that detects changes in heat, sounds, pressure, and other measurements, and sends the information to a controlling device

surveillance
a watch kept over a person, group, or place

terrain
ground or land

LEARN MORE

Books

Ceceri, Kathy. *Robotics: Discover the Science and Technology of the Future*. White River Junction, VT: Nomad Press, 2012.

Gifford, Clive. *Robots*. New York: Atheneum Books for Young Readers, 2008.

Shulman, Mark, and James Buckley. *Robots*. New York: Time for Kids, 2014.

Websites

To learn more about the US military and its resources, visit **booklinks.abdopublishing.com.** These links are routinely monitored and updated to provide the most current information available.

Visit **www.mycorelibrary.com** for free additional tools for teachers and students.

INDEX

ABOUT THE AUTHOR

Carla Mooney is the author of several books for young readers. She loves learning about people, places, and events in history. She lives in Pittsburgh, Pennsylvania, with her husband, three children, and dog.